SHADES

Hues of Life

SAKHI SAHU SINDHWANI

BookLeaf Publishing

India | USA | UK

Made with ❤ on the BookLeaf Publishing Platform
www.bookleafpub.in
www.bookleafpub.com

Dedication

To all the people out there who wander in the world of
poetry to find themselves.

Preface

Initially when I started writing 'Shades' I was unable to write any piece which truly resonated with me. Then I started looking around for stories, inspirations or even something I had read, watched or heard about. I tried weaving it into something meaningful and Shades was born. Writing Shades has been a gratifying journey for me, both as a person as well as a writer. I hope when you read Shades, it gives you joy, insight as well as some motivation for introspection. It is a book filled with scenarios which we have either personally experienced or know someone who has. It is a book of love, power of faith, nostalgia, relationship issues, generational gap and much more.

Happy Reading!

Acknowledgements

I would like to express my deepest gratitude to my Parents for their unwavering love and support. To my spouse, who encouraged me and endured my countless revisions with a smile and to our Daughter who lights up our lives. To my Family and friends who have always been there for me and believed in me. My sincere appreciation goes to my alma mater and my teachers who were instrumental and played a vital role in shaping me. Finally, to the readers who embark on this adventure with me, thank you for giving my creations a home in your mind and hearts.

Delusions

Mirror mirror on the wall,
Are you true or are you false?

Why do you look big;
When you're actually small?

Why do people start to disappear,
As soon as the troubles are near?

Why is that girl crying,
Was it even worth trying?

The road looks deserted and long,
Everything seems to be going wrong.

She thought she could trust you,
But you have changed sides, too.

Nothing seems familiar,
People are further than they appear.

Mirror mirror on the wall,
It is time to take the plunge or be ready for the fall.

Generational Gap

The roots stood strong and firm;
But its branches wanted to squirm.

The roots served as a bind;
However the branches had their own mind.

The roots were getting old;
The branches were unwilling to mould.

The branches paid no heed,
They wanted to plant their own seed.

The branches wanted to sever and fly high;
The roots were not meant for sky.

The branches were in a lot of haste,
Roots thought it was all for a waste.

Soon the weather started to change;
It gave way for some insightful exchange.

The branches could not be bound;
The roots still wanted to hold their ground.

Stumped

I raced back to see the look on your surprised face,
Little did I know that I would be thrown off base.

My eyes burned;
My heart ached;

Who was He?
I thought we'd sit and sip our coffee.

The words blurted out of my mouth,
How could You?
When did You?

Our love began in school;
Was I a fool?

Those love letters,
Seemed to have jitters.

The long walks;

The endless talks;

It is all now in vain,
She looked away when my eyes asked her-
What did you gain?

In that café corner where laughter once brewed,
Now silence lingers, thickening the mood.

In Tandem

The way the rivers meet;
The way old friends greet.

The way two loving hands intertwine;
It seems more than just fine.

The way some people seamlessly blend;
They don't do it to keep up with the 'trend'

The way their eyes lock in a crowd;
It's a silent song and yet so loud.

The way butter melts on a toasted slice;
The way a virtue cuts a vice.

The way the stars twinkle in the night;
The way love illuminates the dark with light

The way two people look at each other;
And there's no need to look any further.

For better or worse

A Cozy bed;
Over a Rosy bed lined with thorns.

A Clear sky;
Over a Starry sky encircled by storm.

An Owned Fiat;
Over a borrowed Ferrari.

A Home brimming with love;
Over a Mansion filled with animosity.

An Unknown well-wisher;
Over a Known Devil.

A genuine laugh;
Over a half-hearted smile.

A Sustainable meal;
Over a Momentary feast.

Feelings that last;
Over fleeting emotions.

Permanent happiness;
Over Temporary joy.

Our lives are timed;
Make it large.

Small things

If only you'd showed up for me,
Instead of gifting me that expensive watch.

It was my birthday;
You should have taken it up by a notch.

I'd rather hear your actual tone;
Than getting a wish from your phone.

I would have preferred a candlelight with just you;
While you threw a fancy party with the who's who.

This is all quite tragic;
Where is that cherished Magic?

If only you had listened;
And not shrugged it off.

If instead of blatantly disregarding me;
You would have given it a thought.

If only you had made tea for me;
Instead of ordering that caramel coffee.

If only you had known-

It is the small things,
That give any relationship its wings.

Haven

I go to my happy place;
I am comfortable with its pace.

Here, there is no crazy race;
Whenever I look around-there's a happy face.

The concern I receive, I feel I don't even need it;
But my people seem to heed about it.

The air feels lighter;
The curtains seem brighter.

It is all hunky dory;
Our lives are weaved into a beautiful story.

I want to sing and dance;
Here, I am no longer afraid of ruining the stance.

There is sweetness in voice;
There is so much poise.

I go to my Happy Place;
It encompasses Hope and Grace.

Chai

I get up,
And I have a few sips,
And instantly my mood uplifts.

It has a quality;
It gives you a surety.

This is your sign;
You are ready to Rise and Shine.

I devour its fragrance;
It's intoxicating.
And suddenly my dopamine
Is skyrocketing.

I can already feel the power;
It's time to take a shower.

For me, tea is not just a beverage;
Instead it is capable of handling my emotional package.

I'd rather sit back alone and relish my tea;
Than find someone to spill the tea.

Tea is a vibe;
You just got to find your tribe.

Becoming

This phase had me in a daze;
Making everything around a haze.

I had a lot of mixed tears;
And all sorts of fears.

It is all so overwhelming;
Becoming a Mother is unending.

I did get a lot of useful advice;
But I was after all, a Novice.

It took some time to soak it all in,
The life after, their cries, but also the cutest grin.

It is but a Rollercoaster ride;
Of highs, lows and sometimes an intense tide.

Your emotions are all charged up;
The only way round is to buckle up.

I see my baby and everything around me fades away;
May you always be protected from a bad day-
I pray,
I pray.

Autumn of Life

I hope when I get old,
You don't become cold.

I hope whether it's day or night,
You never hesitate to become my sight.

I hope when I become weak,
You don't let havoc wreak.

I hope my shoulders never become a burden,
On which you'd sit and roam around the garden.

I gave you more than I could,
It was all for your good.

I hope when I get wrinkles,
Your eyes smile and twinkle.

I hope this is not too much,
I believe our bond is such.

I gave you life;
Don't let anything cause a strife.

The Unsaid

Silence speaks louder than words,
Silence can change your world.

At no cost should Silence be ignored,
It can turn out to be a double edged sword.

Silence is powerful,
It can quickly make happy become dreadful.

Silence sometimes comes with hate,
It can even change your fate.

It screams;
It shouts;

Silence seeks communication,
It desperately wants to change the situation.

In that blaring noise;
Listen to that feeble voice.

It's telling you to express;
You should not suppress.

Before it gets too late, speak up;
Because whatever it is, it's eating you up .

Detached

They failed to notice the lesser talks;
They slowly forgot about their daily walks.

The smiles had started to turn into frowns;
They didn't even know if the other was out of town.

The emotional connect had started to fade away;
Misunderstandings and ego had started to come in the
way.

The equations had become more formal;
Eating meals together was now far from normal.

The phone calls brought some hesitation;
The roots were stemming with underlying frustration.

Initially conflicts were readily resolved- by talking it out;
But now indifferences had started to sprout.

They were walking down a dangerous road;

One which could quickly erode.

Gradually the cracks started to deepen;
And alongwith the distances started to seep in.

It all happens slowly but stealthily;
It requires efforts to ensure love runs in the family.

Implicit

The stolen glances;
The taken chances.

The contagious laughter;
Not giving much thought about life after.

The unspoken messages;
The tender hand brushes.

The mild insinuation;
The uncanny association.

The indirect reference;
Veiled with an obvious preference.

The slight blushing;
Coupled with adrenaline rushing.

The sharing of meals;
Could fall head over heels.

Sometimes love leaves no trace;
You can find love in the most unexpected place.

Good old days

The bonding between cousins;
The never ending carrom sessions.

Happiness for homemade goodies;
Sharing an old plate vis-a-vis fancy cutlery.

Having an old fashioned tea party;
Large hearted people were guaranteed.

Giving unsolicited but useful advice;
Making a social visit without thinking twice.

The essence of flowers over swanky gifts;
Things have undergone a major shift.

The charm of handwritten letters;
Phone is now their biggest competitor.

The meaningful long talks;
Now replaced by faceless chatbots.

Those were the days;
Those were the best ways;

Now there are only vestiges;
To experience those was our privelege.

Hostel

In a city so unknown;
Hostel becomes your home.

The mess becomes your living room;
You see the buds into flowers bloom.

Hostel food has a monotony;
Hostelers never have a full tummy.

Hostel life teaches you so much;
The wardens have their own personal touch.

Hostel did make me nervous;
Initially it was a big circus.

If you are a shy introvert person;
It will push all your exposure buttons.

Hostel gives you a space to be independent;
Your necklace of life gets a cherished pendant.

In Time

They knew it could stir up a controversy;
They shut up and showed the issue some mercy.

They knew things were getting out of hand;
If not dealt with, in trouble they could land.

They kept pushing the difficult conversations;
Slowly demoting endearments to salutations.

The feelings were starting to wither;
The distances were ready to prosper.

Why don't we address the issue when there's still time?
Why do we think expressing is a crime?

Problems don't disappear on their own;
Solution is never to postpone.

Unpleasant talks make the relation stronger;
They make you grow and sustain longer.

What's the point of living together if you can't let your
heart speak?
Give up this game of hide and seek.

Prayer

I pray when I am sad;
Things seem to go from worse to not that bad.

I pray when I am happy;
It helps to keep me calm and not become snappy.

I pray when I am ready;
Things seem to get a little steady.

I pray when I am unprepared;
It makes the rocky path ahead a bit easier to tread.

I pray when I excel;
And the thoughts of a brighter future dwell.

I pray when I fail;
It kickstarts my static boat to sail.

I pray when it gets dark;
With a hope that a new journey is about to embark.

I pray when there's light;
Keeping my blessings in sight;
And trying to keep the things right.

Despite the many obstacles, you can get there,
Alongside your efforts, you just need to make a heartfelt
prayer.

Unperturbed

I was having a bad day;
And I spotted a smiling face.

Suddenly my mood changed;
It made me realize the minority of my pain.

Sometimes we let problems overpower us;
However at times, they do not require that much fuss.

Focus your energy on the positive;
There will always be some or the other negative.

Reasons to ruin your mood are endless;
They are nothing but rentless.

Don't give them so much power;
You need to stop watering that flower.

Life gives you lemons-make a lemonade;
But do not at any cost, let your happiness trade.

Brighten your day with a smile;
In the canvas of life, it is a vital tile.

Fate

He assumed he was in the driver's seat;
Little did he know it was the destiny street.

He had thoroughly done his homework;
But was that enough to make his plans work?

There were a few mistakes;
Life does give you a few retakes.

You think you have it all sorted out;
Before you know, you've reached a roundabout.

You were clear it was meant to be;
Why has it now became a fantasy?

You claimed it to be your end goal;
And suddenly it now had no soul.

You think you know the way to your destination;
And then you land at some off-route station.

There's a limit to having it all figured;
Post that, it's Life's way forward.

Opaque

If only people give words to their thoughts;
It leaves no room for clarity to be sought.

Sometimes people don't mean the things they say;
It's purely out of anger or other emotions at play.

If such is the case, don't wait it out;
Speak your mind and sort it out.

People hear something which they try to process;
This gives lots of opportunities to speculate and guess.

If only they are clear and straightforward in their
speech;
It would not lead to any judgement breach.

More often than not, Ambiguity leads to
misunderstanding;
Before you know it, in your relation, you might be the
only one standing.

Bonds are fragile and need protection;
We should not leave our conversation up for wrongful
dissection.

People thrive on what they listen and read about;
And the mind is cast with shadows of doubt.

When there's scope for interpretation;
It opens the wild gates of imagination;
You can only hope they don't reach the wrong
conclusion.

Navigating healthy relationships requires a great deal of
accountability;
The enemy of which is Ambiguity.

Humanitarian

Humanity is under cloud;
People are punished to think out loud.

The news is buzzing with all things evil;
It seems people have forgotten to be civil.

The world is rife with all sorts of crimes;
Never thought we'd have to encounter such times.

Your known people can no longer be trusted;
Genuineness is now done and dusted.

To be able to live in a safe society looks like a far-fetched
dream;
In a place where every other day people devise
fraudulent schemes.

Wherever we see there is some or the other greed;
Things are taking an ugly turn at full throttle speed.

The world desperately needs a makeover;
It should be done soon before the hope for it is over.

May we only manufacture 'good' in our thoughts factory;
May the air we breathe be filled with camaraderie.

May we all get some useful insight;
Let us always strive to be right.

It is never in vain;
To be more Humane.

www.ingramcontent.com/pod-product-compliance
Lightning Source LLC
Chambersburg PA
CBHW070609160726

48003CB00005B/2189